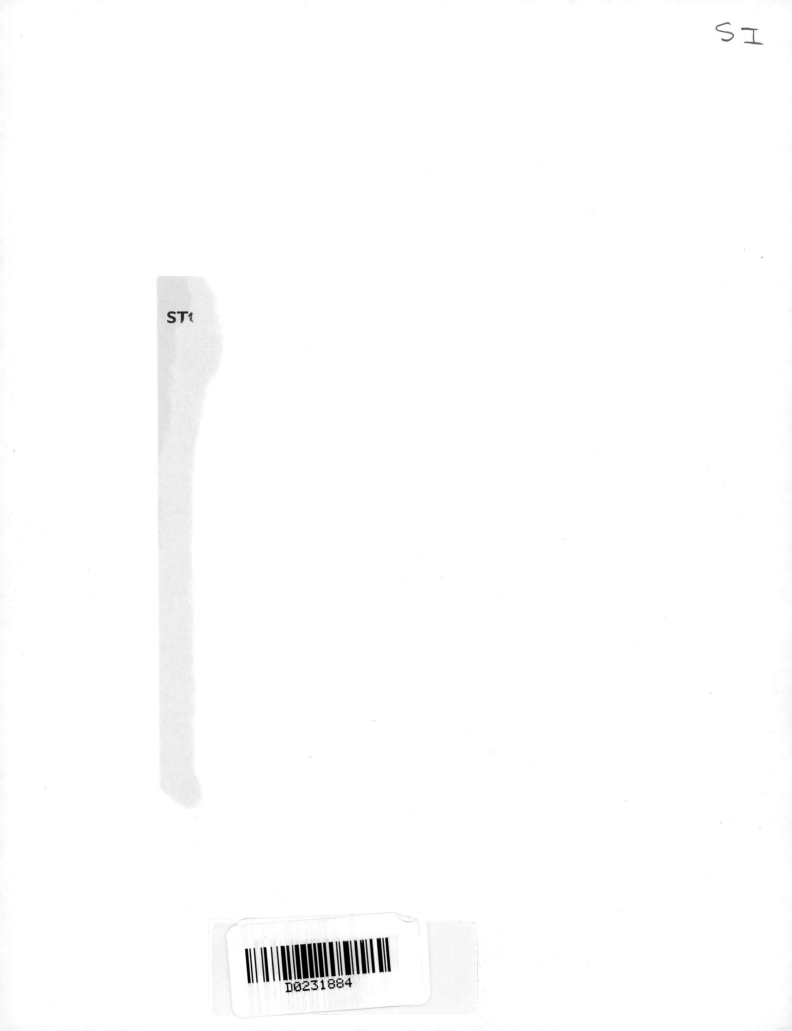

SI

Picture History
of the
20th Century

THE 1920s

Richard Tames

FRANKLIN WATTS
LONDON•SYDNEY

This edition © 2004 Franklin Watts

Franklin Watts
96 Leonard Street
London
EC2A 4XD

Franklin Watts Australia
45-51 Huntley Street
Alexandria
NSW 2015

ISBN 0 7496 5666 2

First published in 1991

Design: K and Co
Editor: Hazel Poole
Picture Research: Sarah Ridley, Ambreen Husain
Printed in Belgium

A CIP catalogue record for this book is available from
the British Library

Photographs: The Architectural Press 43(B); Associated Press/Topham 45(BL);
N. S. Barrett 36(B), 37(T), 37(C); The Bettmann Archive/Hulton-Deutsch 44(BL);
BFI Stills, Posters and Designs 39(T), 39(C); Martin Breese/Retrograph Archive
Collection 13(B), 33(B); Mary Evans Picture Library 9(B), 10(B), 11(C), 11(B),
17(B), 19(B), 21(T), 22(B), 23(B), 24(B), 25(B), 28(T), 29(BL), 36(T), 37(BL),
38(T); Mary Evans/Explorer 32(B); Mary Evans/Steve Rumney 32(T); Ford Motor
Archive 25(T); John Frost Newspapers 19(C); Robert Harding 8(BOTH); Hulton-
Deutsch 12(T), 30(B), 44(BC), 44(BR); The Illustrated London News 20(T);
L'Illustration/Sygma 13(T), 15(B), 16(B), 18(T); Keystone/Sygma 38(B); Kobal
Collection 26(BOTH), 27(ALL), 28(B), 29(T), 29(BR); Robert Opie 24(T), 43(TR);
Popperfoto 6(BOTH), 7(ALL), 9(T), 10(T), 11(T), 12(B), 13(C), 14(BOTH), 15(T),
16(T), 17(T), 17(C), 18(B), 20(B), 23(TL), 23(TR), 31(C), 33(T), 37(BR);
illustration from WINNIE THE POOH copyright E. H. Shephard under the Berne
Convention, reproduced by permission of Curtis Brown, London 39(B); courtesy of
Marie Stopes Clinics 21(C); Topham 19(T), 21(B), 45(BC), 45(BR); The Vintage
Magazine Company 22(T), 31(T), 42(BL), 42(BR), 43(TL); with thanks to the
Visual Arts Library 42(T); reproduced by permission of Warner Chappell Music Ltd
31(B); Val Wilmer 30(T).

cover: Mary Evans Picture Library/Hulton-Deutsch/Kobal Collection
frontispiece: Mary Evans Picture Library

CONTENTS

Introduction

The destruction of World War I gave birth to new nations and enabled others to re-establish their ancient independence. Ireland, after centuries of struggle, at last threw off British rule, but at the cost of partition. Poland, extinguished in the 18th century, was plunged into war almost as soon as it was re-born. Turkey, likewise, arose as a fighting republic out of the wreckage of an empire. Yugoslavia and Czechoslovakia were entirely novel creations, while Lithuania and the other small Baltic states could trace their history back for centuries. The great Dominions, Canada and Australia, had gained in industrial and diplomatic strength from their involvement in the war and began to behave more assertively in international affairs. The most obvious beneficiaries of Europe's blood-letting were, in other words, lesser or peripheral states.

The major combatants of the war, by contrast, had little to celebrate. Britain's victory had enlarged her empire at Germany's expense but cost heavily in shipping sunk, investments sold, trade lost and industries run down or distorted by the needs of war. Returning servicemen had been promised "a land fit for heroes to live in" what they got was unemployment as British manufacturers fought to survive in an international trading system which no longer revolved around London. Meanwhile in India

and Palestine, imperial rule met troublesome resistance. France, drained by her appalling war-time losses, got back the "lost provinces" of Alsace and Lorraine but feared Germany's revenge. Germany, ravaged by civil disorder and inflation, bore the bitterness of defeat and the burden of reparations. Italy felt itself an empty-handed victor and, fearful of revolution, threw up a new kind of political movement, Fascism, which would inspire imitation throughout the continent.

Russia and the United States both turned their backs on Europe. Russia, shattered by war and civil war, strove to build a revolutionary society with traditional instruments of terror. The United States, having inspired the establishment of a "League of Nations" to end international anarchy, declined to join it and turned in on itself to enjoy a decade of unprecedented prosperity.

In the arts and literature, the 1920s was a time of confusion and experiment. Science was less marked by basic advances than by the wider diffusion of its benefits into everyday life through better medical treatment, regular air services and such novelties as frozen food, the wireless and the "talkies". It was a restless decade which constantly surprised itself by promoting unexpected heroes from obscurity such as Valentino, Lindbergh—and Hitler.

Britain in the 1920s

The 1920s did not bring the return to settled prosperity that millions of ex-servicemen had looked for. Although the civil war in Ireland was resolved by the establishment of an "Irish Free State" in 1922, Britain faced determined opposition to its rule elsewhere, in Egypt, Palestine and India.

From 1920 onwards, unemployment mounted as manufacturing industry revealed its loss of competitiveness. The massive coal industry, plagued by fragmented ownership and under-investment, was crucial to the whole economy.

Its problems eventually led to a national crisis – the nine day General Strike of May 1926. This saw Britons back off from revolution but achieved nothing for the miners and led to new laws restricting strike action.

One positive note was that women achieved the vote on the same terms as men in 1928. The rapid diffusion of electric power began a silent revolution in industry, leisure and domestic life, witnessed by the establishment of the BBC and of the Central Electricity Generating Board.

△ (James) Ramsay MacDonald served as Prime Minister of Britain's first Labour governments in 1924 and 1929–31. He reassured the nervous that socialism did not mean revolution but failed to produce new ideas to meet the challenge of a failing economy and long-standing social divisions.

◁ Stanley Baldwin served as Prime Minister in 1923 and 1924–9. A wealthy industrialist, he liked to pose as a plain countryman and is seen here at Chequers, the premier's official rural retreat. Rarely seen without his famous pipe, he stood for calmness in a decade of difficulties.

◁ The 1926 General Strike affected regular bus and train services. Volunteers provided a chaotic substitute while drivers gave lifts to strangers. This scene shows central London during the Strike.

▷ Volunteers of the Organisation for the Maintenance of Supplies move milk churns in 1926.

◁ The end of the Great War was followed by a renewal of trouble in Ireland as nationalists fought to create an independent state. The Royal Irish Constabulary Auxiliaries were mostly ex-servicemen. Dressed in a mixture of discarded army uniforms, they were known as the "Black and Tans".

A New International Order

World War I began as a punitive expedition to save small nations such as Serbia and Belgium from the aggression of Germany and its allies. It ended as a crusade to "make the world safe for democracy" and to end war itself.

The peace-makers who gathered in Paris in 1919 set themselves two contradictory aims – to create a secure framework for a new international order and to humiliate and punish the defeated powers. High hopes were pinned on the newly-established League of Nations, but it was gravely weakened from the outset by the refusal of the United States to join. Attempts to make Germany "pay" for war damage through massive reparations only succeeded in disrupting the recovery of the post-war European economy and were finally abandoned in 1932.

Significant but unspectacular progress was made, however, in important aspects of international co-operation such as the collection of statistics, the treatment of refugees and promotion of labour rights. The inauguration of regular airline services between nations helped to bring them closer together but also raised fears of aerial warfare.

How The War – And Four Peace Treaties Changed The Map Of Europe

Lost by Germany 1919

Saar: League of Nations control

Austria-Hungary until 1918

Former territory of Imperial Russia

△ World War I destroyed three multi-national empires – Russian, Ottoman and Austro-Hungarian. Successor states were troubled by minority problems.

◁ Palace of hope – the League of Nations building at Geneva in Switzerland. The League failed to end international conflicts but did much valuable work nonetheless.

▷ The Kellogg-Briand pact was signed by 15 nations in 1928 and eventually ratified by a total of 62. The signatories pledged to renounce war as a means of settling disputes but provided no means of punishing lapses or preventing undeclared wars.

▽ Each newly independent nation advertised its sovereignty by issuing its own stamps and coins and adopting a national anthem and flag. Fierce national pride and the right to erect tariff barriers made the prospects for international co-operation less hopeful.

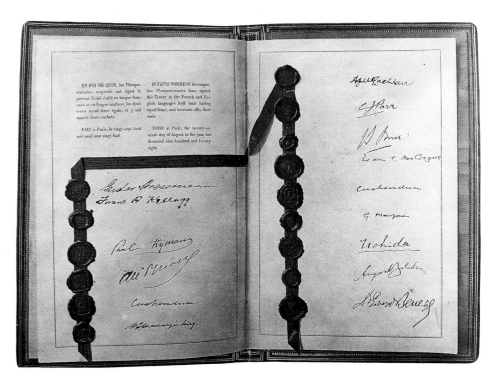

▽ The Washington Disarmament Conference of 1921–22 scaled down the strength of the world's major navies, required the United States, France, Britain and Japan to respect each other's Pacific possessions and outlawed the use of gas in warfare. The 1927 Geneva Conference failed to cut navies still further.

Lenin's Russia

By mid-1920, the hastily-created Red Army had ensured the victory of the Bolsheviks over the "Whites", a loose coalition of anti-Communists supported by western governments. A brief but bloody war with newly-independent Poland was followed by widespread famine, bringing the economy to the verge of collapse. Against this gloomy background, a Union of Soviet Socialist Republics was finally established in 1922. Meanwhile, a "New Economic Policy" was swiftly introduced to reverse earlier attempts at wholesale nationalisation and overcome a complete collapse in production and food supplies.

Lenin's death was then followed by a power struggle in which Stalin overcame Trotsky to emerge by 1929 as a supreme dictator, pledged to the building of "socialism in one country" rather than fomenting worldwide revolution as Trotsky had wished. This was to be done through enforced industrialisation and the collectivisation of agriculture and by mass-terror if necessary.

△ Leon Trotsky was the creator of the Red Army which gave the Bolsheviks victory in the civil war. (Note he is wearing a uniform.) Although he was Lenin's chief lieutenant, he was eventually forced into exile in 1929 and killed on Stalin's orders in 1940.

◁ In 1920, Poland tried to take the Ukraine. Here, the Poznan Regiment waits to attack Kiev, which fell on May 7. Counterattacks took the Russians to the edge of Warsaw, where French support helped the Poles drive them back. The 1921 Treaty of Riga re-defined frontiers.

◁ Nikolai Bukharin, seen here addressing a Moscow crowd in 1922, never held a top political post but had great influence as editor of the party newspaper *Pravda (Truth)*. He was denounced in 1928 and finally executed after a "show-trial" in 1938.

▷ The cumulative effects of war followed by a civil war led to a disastrous famine in the Volga region in 1922.

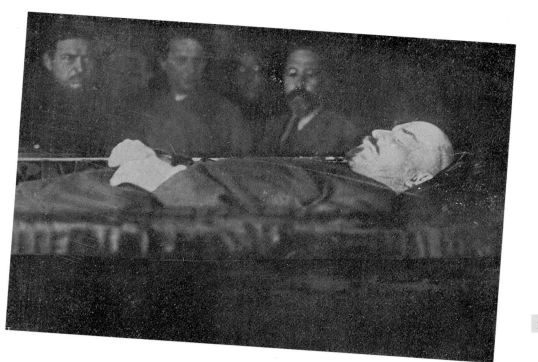

▷ Lenin, lying in state after his death in 1924. His belief that "there is room for other parties only in jail" gave a monopoly of power to the Communists but failed to secure a smooth succession to his personal control over it. In an atheist country, his mausoleum became a focus for personal pilgrimage and collective rituals.

Mussolini's Italy

Italy came out of World War I on the winning side but her meagre territorial gains seemed to many patriots a poor reward for her sacrifices. Economic dislocation threatened social revolution and favoured political extremism. In 1919, ex-socialist Benito Mussolini launched his Fascio di Combattimento, an anti-socialist militia inspired by ultra-nationalism and with a disposition to violence. His muddled programme of reform at least promised decisive action and attracted many ex-soldiers to the ranks of the Fascists. Having bluffed and bullied his way to power, Mussolini proceeded to eliminate opposition to his rule and suppress civil liberties. Parliamentary debate was replaced by parades and slogans "Mussolini is always right", proclaimed one. Another simply required, "Believe, Obey, Fight".

▽ Ex-newspaperman Mussolini after seizing control of Rome in a bloodless coup on 29 October, 1922.

△ Cyclists wearing the cockerel-feather helmets of crack Italian mountain troops hail their country's leader, "Il Duce".

◁ Mussolini rides in a procession to celebrate the tenth anniversary of his seizure of power. Jack-booted Fascists give the party's raised-arm salute. The ruins of the Roman Coliseum serve as a reminder of the past glories Mussolini sought to revive – or at least to exploit. In practice, Italy's military power was limited by its economic backwardness.

◁ A special postage stamp celebrates an exhibition held in Alto Adige, a northern province acquired after World War I. The local German-speaking minority resented incorporation in the Italian state. Note the "fasces", the bundle of rods, symbolising unity, from which Fascism took its name.

△ Pope Pius XI at his desk in the Vatican. In 1929, Mussolini achieved a major diplomatic success with the signing of the Lateran Treaty by which Italy recognised the independence of the Vatican state and accepted Roman Catholicism as the sole official religion of the country.

Weimar Germany

On 11 November, 1918, Germany accepted Allied terms for an armistice and the Kaiser, the "supreme warlord", fled into exile in neutral Holland. With her army reeling under the hammer-blows of co-ordinated attacks by the advancing Allies, her navy in a state of open mutiny and her civilian population on the edge of starvation or revolt, Germany had nothing left to fight with, yet alone fight for.

Yet, when she sued for peace, no Allied army had invaded her territory. Thus was born the legend of the "dolchstoss", the "stab in the back", which alleged that Germany had never been defeated, only betrayed. And the betrayers were identified as the liberals and socialists who had signed the armistice and established a new republic based on a constitution drawn up in the elegant town of Weimar. For many Germans, the regime of the "November criminals" could command no loyalty.

Five years of political turmoil preceded an unsteady economic recovery and were accompanied by a flowering of avant-garde art, music and drama which seemed to traditional patriots clear proof of the degeneration of the times. The onset of depression after 1929 sealed the fate of an unloved regime.

△ Dr. Walther Rathenau, who served as minister of reconstruction and foreign minister before being assassinated by right-wing extremists after engineering the Russo-German Treaty of Rapallo which developed co-operation between the Soviet Union and Weimar Germany.

◁ French troops in the Ruhr in 1923. The presence of foreign forces on German soil proved to angry patriots the weakness of the Weimar regime. In the end, German reparation payments were to be scaled down by international agreement.

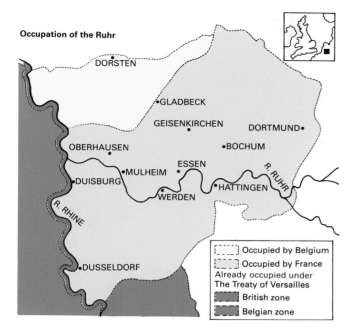

Occupation of the Ruhr

DORSTEN

GLADBECK

GEISENKIRCHEN   DORTMUND•

OBERHAUSEN   •BOCHUM

MULHEIM   ESSEN

DUISBURG   R. RUHR

WERDEN   HATTINGEN

R. RHINE

•DUSSELDORF

Occupied by Belgium
Occupied by France
Already occupied under
The Treaty of Versailles
British zone
Belgian zone

△ The Treaty of Versailles imposed heavy reparations payments on Germany to punish aggression and finance reconstruction. When Germany defaulted, France and Belgium sent troops into the industrial Ruhr.

▷ Adolf Hitler in prison at the fortress of Landsberg-Am-Lech after the failure of his 1923 beer-hall putsch. He was allowed many visitors and gained valuable publicity by writing *Mein Kampf (My Struggle)*.

◁ The strain of paying reparations undermined the German currency from 1922 onwards. Here, 8,000 DM are seen as the equivalent of $1. The occupation of the Ruhr in 1923 led the local population to respond with passive resistance which hampered the invaders but also damaged the economy leading to a final collapse of the currency. A new "rentenmark", introduced in November 1923, could be exchanged for one trillion old marks. The currency collapse wiped out the savings of the middle classes but enabled some speculators to make fortunes and acquire popular hatred.

Men of Power

The shock waves of World War I continued long after the actual fighting ended. Political instability, together with the new power of mass media to focus attention on dramatic actions and striking personalities, created situations in which a strong leader could appear to offer decisive solutions to the many problems. Lenin and Mussolini offered clear models at opposite ends of the political spectrum.

The break-up of the immense multi-national Austro-Hungarian empire made Eastern Europe especially vulnerable to authoritarian regimes. In Hungary, Admiral Miklós Horthy led counter-revolutionary forces against the communist uprising of Bela Kun and ruled the country for the next 25 years. Poland, Yugoslavia and Greece proved to be equally vulnerable while Albania saw the adventurer Ahmed Bey Zogu transform himself from president into king in 1928.

Even some democracies seemed to find security under the guidance of a single dominating individual. In newly-established Czechoslovakia, Thomas Masaryk, leader of the independence movement, ruled as president from 1918 to 1935. Greece exchanged monarchy for turmoil until Prime Minister Venizelos brought some stability (1928–32).

△ Marshal Józef Pilsudski, hero of the Russo-Polish war, was head of state of newly-independent Poland until 1922. Impatient with democracy, he established a military dictatorship in 1926 which lasted until his death in 1935.

◁ Reza Shah Pahlevi with his infant son in 1926. A Cossack adventurer, he seized power in Iran in 1921, proclaimed himself Shah in 1925 and, taking Atatürk as his model, attempted a rapid modernisation of the state and economy.

◁ Alexander Karadjordjevic on his wedding day in 1922. Having served as Regent for his father, Peter I, from 1918 to 1921, he ruled over the kingdom of Serbs, Croats and Slovenes during a phase of disorderly democracy before proclaiming a dictatorship and renaming the country Yugoslavia (United Slavs) in 1929.

◁ Miguel Primo de Rivera seized control of Spain with military backing in 1923, ruling as effective dictator until economic failures forced his resignation in 1930.

△ Mustafa Kemal created the modern Turkish republic out of the ruins of the Ottoman Empire. Taking the surname of "Atatürk" ("Father of the Turks"), he promoted western culture enthusiastically.

Hitting the Headlines

World War I and the political convulsions that followed it not only stimulated demand for news among readers, but also led to the extension of a worldwide news-gathering network of reporters, photographers and wire-services. Regular coverage of sport and business, plus the addition of "women's pages" and even children's features made newspapers bulkier than before, the extra pages being paid for by the increase in advertising.

In 1921, photographs of mysterious depressions in the snows of the Himalayas started the legend of "Big Foot", which, like the Loch Ness Monster, provided the papers with a story that would run for years. Newspapers themselves "created" news by sponsoring competitions, exhibitions and attempts to break sporting or speed records. Yet, as late as 1928, the BBC could announce instead of a regular bulletin – "There is no news today".

Nevertheless, radio and cinema brought news to the public more swiftly and more dramatically than ever before, provoking newspapers into a more visual style of news presentation.

△ The British mountaineer George Mallory leading an assault on Everest, the world's highest peak. Note the absence of breathing apparatus and special protective clothing. Mallory died in the course of his third attempt. He may have reached the summit.

◁ The great Kanto earthquake of September 1923 killed some 100,000 people in Tokyo and the port of Yokohama and rendered two million homeless. Flooding, looting and cholera followed, but the Japanese capital was swiftly rebuilt. The picture shows survivors in makeshift shacks.

▷ Franco-Spanish forces use a heliograph to communicate in the Rif Mountains of Morocco. The revolt of Abd-al-Krim against colonial rule took five years to suppress. After 20 years in detention, he escaped to live in retirement as an inspiration for the next generation of Arab nationalists.

Daily News front page — "RED PLOT AGAINST BRITAIN."

◁ The revelation of the "Zinoviev letter" on the eve of the 1924 election sank Labour's chances. It later proved to be a forgery.

▽ China proved to be a convenient source of foreign news – vast but divided, exotic but too weak to threaten western interests.

The "Red" Menace Among the Yellow Men
THE CHINESE STRIKERS AND THEIR CITIZEN TRIBUNALS

CHINESE SERVANTS ARRESTED BY THE REDS
armed picket of the "Red" army holding up boys who attempted to reach Hong Kong, which the boycott has placed out of bounds.

WOMEN PRISONERS AND THEIR ARMED GUARDS
Two girl prisoners about to be tried by the strikers' court, an institution introduced by the Russians.

The New Woman

World War I shattered the myth of feminine frailty. In Britain, political leaders who had once denied women the vote admitted that the war could not have been won without their efforts and accepted their claim to full citizenship. In 1919, the American Nancy Astor became the first woman to take a seat in the British House of Commons.

Even the women who returned readily to the ideal of domestic bliss did so with the conviction that they were more educated and more worldly-wise than their mothers had ever been. Cigarette-smoking, the use of make-up and a knowledge of birth control were almost, if not quite, respectable.

The number of domestic servants fell drastically compared with the pre-war period. Young girls preferred the less restrictive conditions of work in offices, shops and factories which war production had made familiar to many. Able to delegate less, middle-class housewives took a new interest in labour-saving devices like the vacuum cleaner and electric iron and time-saving "convenience foods" like custard powder, tinned fruits and packeted breakfast cereals. New magazines like *Good Housekeeping* (1922) helped them to cope.

△ Amelia Earhart, the first woman to fly the Atlantic – as a passenger in 1928 and later solo in 1932. Women pilots were the supreme example of the fearless, technically capable woman.

◁ Seven of the House of Commons' eight women Members of Parliament in 1924. Lady Astor is third from the left and Margaret Bondfield, who was to become the first woman Cabinet minister, is on the far right. In 1928, women were given the same voting rights as men.

◁ Marie Stopes opened Britain's first birth control clinic in 1921 and tried to spread knowledge of family planning techniques through her books and pamphlets. This mobile caravan offered "free practical instruction" from a reassuringly proper uniformed nurse. Many churchmen preached against this new trend.

▽ Swim-suited "bathing beauties" at Atlantic City in 1922. Compared to 10 years earlier, the costumes were daringly revealing.

Take to the Air

One of the more constructive outcomes of the Paris Peace Conference of 1919 was the signing of an International Convention for Aerial Navigation, which gave free passage over their internal air space to all aircraft of the countries involved.

At the end of the Great War, there were surplus planes and pilots looking for work in the untested field of civil aviation. In particular, in the United States, many took part in dare-devil stunts for "flying circuses" or, less romantically, flew crop-dusters for farmers.

In Europe, eager efforts to set up regular air services between major cities led to cut-throat competition as governments, for reasons of strategy and prestige, subsidised new commercial carriers. In 1924, Britain's four fledgling airlines merged to form Imperial Airways, with official backing of £1 million over 10 years. It concentrated on developing routes to India via the Middle East, using specially designed aircraft capable of heavier pay-loads and much longer distances.

In May 1926, Americans Byrd and Bennett were the first men to fly over the North Pole. Two days later, Norwegian Amundsen's airship repeated the feat.

GREAT BRITAIN · HOLDER ·
Nº OF WINS: 3
YEARS: 1914, 1922, 1927.

U.S.A.
Nº OF WINS: 2
YEARS: 1923, 1925.

THE
JACQUES SCHNEIDER MARITIME TROPHY
Presented in 1912 to the AÉRO CLUB DE FRANCE by M. Jacques Schneider for an International Aviation Competition under Rules approved by the Federation Aeronautique Internationale

ITALY RUNNER-UP
Nº OF WINS: 3
YEARS: 1920, 1921, 1926.

FRANCE
Nº OF WINS: 1
YEAR: 1913.

△ In 1913, the French flying enthusiast Jacques Schneider presented a trophy for an annual competition for seaplanes, consisting of an air race and seaworthiness trials. The contest boosted both public interest and technical progress in flying during the 1920s.

◁ Sir Alan Cobham, seen here landing on the Thames at Westminster on his return from a record-breaking two way flight to Australia in 1926. Record flights were important in testing the feasibility of long-haul routes but did little to convince potential passengers that flying was a routine form of travel.

△ A de Bathezat experimental helicopter in actual flight in 1922. A helicopter able to carry a person had been built in France as early as 1907 but it was not until the 1930s that models suitable for actual commercial and military use were developed, chiefly by the Russian-American Igor Sikorsky.

▽ The German airship *Graf Zeppelin* entering its New Jersey hangar after crossing the Atlantic in 1924. Count (Graf) von Zeppelin built his first rigid airship in 1900 and by 1914, the airship had carried 35,000 people without accident. The 1930 crash of the British *R101* came as a severe setback to airship use.

△ On 21 May, 1927, Charles Lindbergh of Minnesota became the first man to fly the Atlantic solo, non-stop. Loaded down with petrol, his *Spirit of St. Louis* lurched into the sky at Long Island to touch down 33 hours later at Le Bourget, Paris. He won $25,000 and undying fame.

The Motor Revolution

Millions of men learned to drive during World War I and post-war sales of army surplus made vehicles easily available to civilians.

Europe's first mass-produced car, the French Citroen Type A, was introduced in 1919 and in 1922 the "bull-nosed" Morris Oxford was launched in Britain as a cheap family car. Priced at £170, it represented more than one third of an annual income for a "well-off" middle class family. However, it could be bought for a downpayment of £25 followed by weekly payments of £2. Its rival, the Austin 7, boasted the speed of a big car (50 mph) in a compact and economical (40 mpg) design.

By 1924 there were 1.3 million cars and lorries on the roads in Britain and by 1925, Morris were proclaiming a new sales record of 4,380 cars delivered in a single month. Sales promotions included a year's fully comprehensive insurance (worth £11) and a choice of colours (blue or grey). In 1928, the American giant General Motors took car design in a new direction when it appointed Harley Earl as head of its new "art and Color" section. It was now clearly recognised that the customer wanted not merely efficiency but style as well.

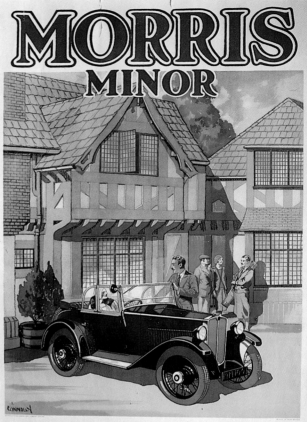

MORRIS MINOR

THREE-SPEED TWO-SEATER
£100
ex Works

FOUR-SPEED MODELS
from **£105**
ex Works

△ This popular "run-about" is clearly aimed at a middle class market of golf-playing suburbanites. Like many 1920s models it was driven open or with a soft top – draughty in winter.

◁ An overturned car draws a curious crowd which the uniformed chauffeur turns his back on. Poor roadmarking and streetlighting and the absence of traffic-lights and driving tests meant that accident rates were high despite a low volume of traffic.

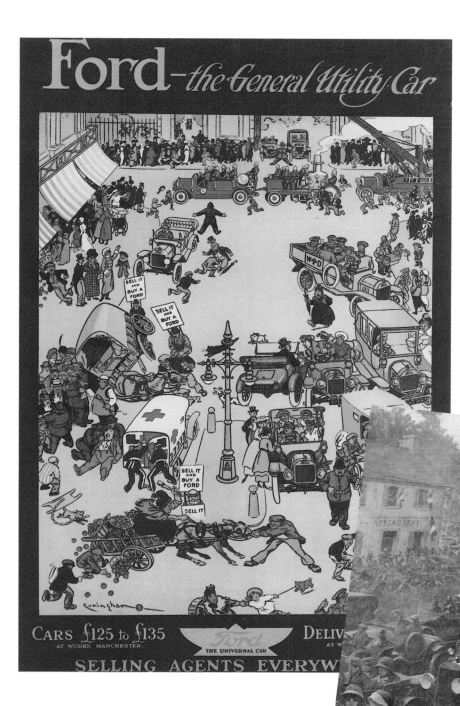

◁ American motor company Ford opened its first production line factory overseas at Old Trafford near Manchester before World War I. In the 1920s, it began to build a huge assembly works at Dagenham, to the east of London where the Thames gave deep-water access for ships. This new plant enabled it to meet the challenge of large-scale domestic British rivals like Morris and Austin.

▷ A French magazine illustrates the jam of motor traffic caused by spectators at a motor-racing circuit. Although only the very rich could participate in motor racing, it was a sensational sport for spectators. The handbuilt racing cars of Italian Ettore Bugatti set new standards of engineering excellence which were eventually to influence the design and construction of the ordinary car.

The Movies

The cinema came of age in the 1920s and Hollywood confirmed its position as the "dream factory" of the English-speaking world. It was there that fame and fortune could be found, along with movie "moguls" – producers like Cecil B. De Mille who conceived and financed pictures.

In Russia, France and Germany, it was the directors who led the way in developing film as a serious art form. The epic *Napoleon*, directed by Frenchman Abel Gance, appeared in 1927 and is now recognized as a masterpiece of silent film technique. But in the very same year, *The Jazz Singer* broke new ground by incorporating the first live screen dialogue.

1928 saw Walt Disney's first successful sound picture *Steamboat Willie*, featuring his most famous creation, Mickey (originally Mortimer!) Mouse. In the same year, the comedy duo of Stan Laurel and Oliver Hardy made no less than four feature films to keep up with public demand.

As cinema-going became a regular weekly habit on both sides of the Atlantic, it also became a powerful agency for spreading American slang, dance and fashion worldwide.

△ **Charlie Chaplin with Jackie Coogan in *The Kid* (1921), which Chaplin also directed. He developed a highly visual style of acting which combined a skilful use of gesture and timing with brilliant athletic skills, enabling him to contrast pathos and slapstick, moving stories forward without dialogue.**

◁ **The establishment of the Academy Awards showed the maturing of cinema as an industry confident of its own technical and artistic standards. At first a local initiative of the Los Angeles area, the Awards soon acquired international status. The name "Oscar" came from a secretary whose uncle bore a striking resemblance to the statuette—so his name was given to it.**

◁ The thrilling chariot race from *Ben Hur* (1926).

▽ A German poster for the Russian film *The Battleship Potemkin* (1925).

△ Sheet music for tunes from *The Jazz Singer* (1927), starring Al Jolson, a Russian immigrant whose real name was Asa Yoelson.

▷ Walt Disney with Mickey Mouse dolls in 1929. This pioneered a trend to franchising goods based on film successes.

27

The Stars

Whether or not it was their original intention, the film studios of the 1920s found that they had created "stars" whom the public would pay to see – even if the film itself did not appeal much. They remained stars just as long as they kept their popularity in a notoriously high-risk industry. It was therefore desirable that these public figures should behave accordingly. For as long as they worked obediently they were paid well, but if they showed too much independence of mind or became involved in scandal, they could find their career finished overnight – such was the fate of comedy star Roscoe "Fatty" Arbuckle.

Compliance was therefore more important than outstanding talent. Studio publicity offices enhanced the stars' earning power by feeding bits of gossip to magazines targeted at "starry-eyed" fans. Lavish homes and extravagant parties gave them a larger-than-life image which captured the hearts of film-goers on both sides of the Atlantic. Many fantasized about looking like a film star. The various imitated fashions, hair styles and make-up showed the impact of these fantasies. The 1927 off-screen romance of on-screen lovers John Gilbert and Swedish actress Greta Garbo was another sensational example of reality imitating fantasy.

RUDOLPH VALENTINO & VILMA BANKY.
IN "THE SON OF THE SHEIK".
ALLIED ARTISTS PICTURE.
'FAMOUS CINEMA STAR' SERIES.
236.P.
BEAGLES' POSTCARDS

△ Rudolph Valentino starring in *The Son of the Sheik*, a sequel to *The Sheik* which shot him to stardom in 1922. Valentino's death in 1926 from peritonitis was followed by a showy funeral with emotional scenes from devoted fans.

◁ The star who out-lasted them all. More than 50 years after his first appearance on screen, spinach-eating Popeye was still going strong. The appeal of cartoon films, with their ingenious visual humour, went beyond the boundaries of time, space and language.

◁ Timid-looking comedian Harold Lloyd specialised in daring slapstick stunts which were sometimes as dangerous as they looked. Silent acting required many stars to develop athletic skills to make their impact.

"Buster" Keaton (below) in *Sherlock Junior.* Known as "Frozen Face", he was a master of timing and gesture. The ones who got away (below left). Swashbuckling Douglas Fairbanks and Mary Pickford joined with Charlie Chaplin to create "United Artists" as a new company outside of major studio control.

The Jazz Age

It was said that if you needed to ask what jazz was, you wouldn't understand the answer. Jazz allegedly spoke to the emotions, not the intellect; the feet, not the brain. It developed around the turn of the century in the southern states of America, drawing on black work songs, spirituals and other musical forms whose harmonies and rhythms were of African and, to a lesser extent, Latin American inspiration.

Not until the 1920s did it attract attention outside its region of birth, spreading north and west and being imitated and adapted by white musicians. Of these, the most famous was Paul Whiteman, a disillusioned classical musician whose band's first record, *Whispering/Japanese Sandman*, sold two million copies. Whiteman offered his listeners well-drilled orchestration, punctuated with brief "hot" interludes, thrown in to liven the action. It might have been novel, but anyone who had actually experienced New Orleans or a Harlem nightclub knew that it wasn't jazz. The jazz of the "dives" and "speakeasies" aroused fear and fury in the self-appointed defenders of respectable society and conventional cultural standards. They denounced jazz as "primitive", an incitement to sin and an accompaniment to crime. Jazz certainly got music talked about!

△ Louis (Daniel) Armstrong ("Satchmo-Satchelmouth") was already billed as "the world's greatest trumpeter" by the late 1920s. Emerging in New Orleans, he transferred to Chicago after 1922 and recorded with his own band, the "Hot Five". His genius for improvisation boosted the role of the soloist.

◁ Edward Kennedy ("Duke") Ellington with the all-black big band he formed in 1918. An outstanding pianist, he also excelled as an arranger and composer of such standards as *Mood Indigo*. From 1927 to 1932, he starred at Harlem's celebrated Cotton Club.

◁ A fantasy celebration of the "big band" sound suggesting glamour, elegance, romance and the dinner-jacketed high-life of the social elite. Spectacle on this scale represented major commercial investment and therefore offered bland adaptations of the "hot" music found in fringe night clubs. Note the all-white cast.

△ British-born violinist Yehudi Menuhin, seen here at the age of 13, made his debut in San Francisco at age 7. The child prodigy went on to a long career as a performer and teacher.

◁ *Rhapsody in Blue* by George Gershwin baffled critics when it crossed the bounds of colour and tradition to blend jazz with the classical approach.

31

Dance, Dance, Dance

Some saw the scale of the dance craze of the 1920s as an unconscious affirmation of life and gaiety against the gruesome and haunting memories of World War I. Others argued that the sheer monotony of most routine jobs and the drabness of city life made it quite natural that young people should want to dress up and go out with others amid bright lights and bright music.

Jack Payne, leader of the Savoy Orpheans, Britain's most popular dance band, had a simpler answer for the popularity of syncopated music – that it was cheerful and "we all want to be happy."

Mastery of the latest dance craze was a sure way of winning popularity among young people. It was perhaps no coincidence that the globe-trotting playboy Prince of Wales numbered the foxtrot among his well-publicised personal accomplishments.

In 1923, a craze for dance marathons swept America. Promoters offered big money prizes and contestants danced for 40 or 50 hours, until they literally dropped.

Dance-halls became the most popular places for young people to meet future marriage partners.

△ Most of the new dances began in America and had their roots in off-beat rhythms derived from African music through the black community. They spread to Europe via the cinema, supported by records, sheet music, magazine articles and dance handbooks or the exhibitions of trend-setting professionals

◁ The controversial Isadora Duncan developed a style of barefoot dancing based on "natural impulses" and modelled on the inspiration of classical Greek art. Less popular in her native America than in Europe, she also founded a school in Berlin and made many visits to Russia. Her personal life was marked by open love affairs, the tragic loss of her children and her own bizarre death.

▷ Frank Farnum, creator of the "Charleston", demonstrates the new dance with the help of one of his pupils. When it arrived in Britain, it was denounced as dangerous and provoked a newspaper campaign to ban it. Dance halls even put up notices asking their patrons to "Please Charleston Quietly".

◁ If the Charleston was intended to be outrageous fun, the sinuous, elegant tango from Argentina was equally clearly intended to be romantic. Note the high-fashion dress of the dancers, despite the fact that they are supposed to be at an afternoon tea dance, rather than at a nightclub in the early hours of the morning. The slower pace of the tango made it attractive to older dancers or as an interval item between faster numbers.

Fashion

High fashion in the 1920s was dominated by the idea of liberation. During World War I, women had taken men's jobs in factories and on farms. They soon proved, to themselves as well as others, that they could do more and earn more than men had ever thought possible. When the war ended, many discarded their uniforms and working clothes, but were eager to hang on to their new-found independence.

The Paris designer "Coco" Chanel led the way in adopting masculine fabrics such as jersey, flannel, tweed and corduroy and introducing "practical" garments like the trench-coat, sweater and cardigan as high-fashion elements for women. On the other hand, make-up became respectable for women, other than actresses, to use in emphasising their femininity.

The trend towards shorter skirts gave a new importance to stockings and shoes as fashion items. Rayon – known as "artificial silk" and used as a substitute for that expensive material – became available at the end of the decade and was at first almost exclusively used for stockings.

Naturally, such radical changes provoked criticism. In Italy, bishops banned bare-legged women from church. In Britain, doctors alleged short skirts caused puffy, chafed legs.

"I'm too shy to sit on your knee - but I don't mind sitting on your OXFORDS!"

△ "Oxford Bags" originated among the wealthy students of that university.

▽ A Harrods' permanent wave for short hair cost 4 guineas – a month's wage for a shop girl.

▷ A French advertisement for swimwear. Rubber swimming caps were first of all used for the very practical purpose of protecting expensive hair styles from the water, but soon became multi-coloured fashion accessories in their own right. Sun-tanning became a new craze among the young rich, showing that they had the leisure to do nothing in summer and go south in winter.

△ The "New Woman" of the 1920s favoured the active life and adopted masculine styles for riding or driving. Note the man's soft felt hat and immaculate "spats" worn over stylish shoes. Headgear was still thought essential to complete any outfit.

▷ "I remember you when you were in long skirts", the fashionable old gentleman tells the young "flapper". Many new fashions seemed to turn established ideas upside down. Note that both of them are wearing gloves and carrying canes.

Sport

Sport became big business in the 1920s as radio outside broadcasting made it possible for anyone to "listen in" on a great event. The very predictability of sporting fixtures helped newspapers in their planning and provided a steady flow of dramatic pictures and complex records and statistics to fill their pages and give readers something to argue about. Growing popular interest in sport as a spectator activity expanded the scale of each event. World heavyweight boxing champion Jack Dempsey drew crowds of over one million people between 1919 and 1926.

1923 saw the opening of New York's huge Yankee Stadium and of London's Wembley Stadium which could hold 100,000 spectators. They could see not only soccer but also tennis, boxing, ice hockey and greyhound racing, a new sport in which the lighting, totalisator and hare all showed the growing importance of electricity.

Rewards also got bigger. In 1925, college football hero Red Grange joined the Chicago Bears – for $3,000 a game.

△ Mounted police thwart a potential disaster as the crowd spills on to the pitch before the 1923 FA Cup Final at Wembley Stadium. Soccer's status as the national sport was confirmed by the presence of King George V.

◁ Fashion-conscious Frenchwoman Suzanne Lenglen brought a new athleticism to women's tennis and was unbeaten in seven years of tournament play, turning professional for $100,000 in 1926 after winning Wimbledon six times.

▷ At the 1928 Olympic Games, Paavo Nurmi (centre), the "Flying Finn", confirmed his status as the world's greatest middle-distance runner.

▽ The legendary Jack Hobbs at the peak of his career in 1926. Between 1905 and 1934 he set two records which were never surpassed. Swimmer Johnny Weissmuller (below right), the first man to swim 100 metres under one minute, won Olympic medals before a film career as Tarzan. Scottish missionary Eric Liddell (bottom right) refused to run on a Sunday at the 1924 Paris Olympics.

MR JACK HOBBS.

by George Belcher

See where he stands, the Nation's Hope and Pride,
Calmly defiant of the Other Side.
Great nobs their records yield to greater nobs;
One only rival threatens Hobbs. That's Hobbs.

Readers and Writers

The experiences of World War I provoked surprisingly little significant British writing until the end of the decade when two very personal accounts by leading poets appeared – *Memoirs of a Fox-Hunting Man* by Siegfried Sassoon and *Goodbye to all That* by Robert Graves.

New ideas in literature were represented by the movement known as "modernism" which abandoned straightforward narrative and external description of characters and action in favour of radical shifts of style and viewpoint. Leading writers of this movement were Virginia Woolf (*To the Lighthouse*), James Joyce (*Ulysses*) and Franz Kafka (*The Trial*).

In poetry, new directions were charted by T. S. Eliot and Rainer Maria Rilke. Writers who worked within existing conventions included the hugely popular John Galsworthy (*The Forsyte Saga*) and the young master of black comedy Evelyn Waugh (*Decline and Fall*).

Important new talents emerged from America – Scott Fitzgerald (*The Great Gatsby*), Sinclair Lewis (*Main Street*) and Ernest Hemingway (*A Farewell to Arms*).

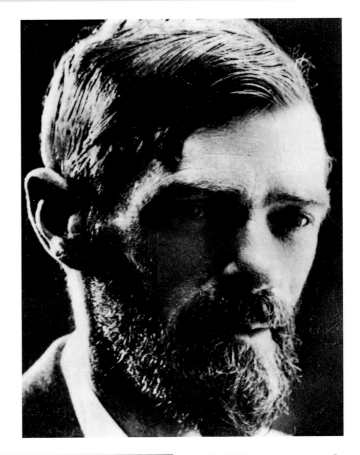

△ D. H. Lawrence seemed to many to represent the modern writer – self-tortured and determined to outrage. During the 1920s he lived in Australia, New Mexico and Italy, seeking the warmth as his health steadily worsened.

◁ Adolf Hitler's *Mein Kampf (My Struggle)* was written during his imprisonment after the failure of his attempted Munich Putsch. A rambling mixture of self-justifying autobiography, cynical political analysis and anti-Semitic propaganda, it was destined to cast a long shadow over the next 20 years of world history.

▷ More than 50 years after they were published, two of the decade's major novels were turned into full-length feature films – F. Scott Fitzgerald's *The Great Gatsby*, a critique of a world of glittering emptiness, and E. M. Forster's *A Passage to India* (below), a study of friendship and racial tension.

▽ Christopher Robin puts Eeyores's tail back in place while Winnie the Pooh looks on encouragingly. A. A. Milne's immortal characters continued to delight each generation of children for the rest of the century.

Science and Medicine

The great medical advance of the decade came in 1928 with Alexander Fleming's discovery of penicillin – the first major antibiotic. It was to take 15 years, however, before a practical method of large-scale manufacture was to be developed at Oxford by the Australian pathologist Howard Florey and his team. A more immediate result was seen with the isolation of the hormone insulin by the Canadians Banting and Best in 1921. This helped to revolutionise the treatment of diabetes.

1922 also saw the award of the Nobel Prize for Chemistry to the Dane Niels Bohr for his research into the structure of the atom. But, again, the full significance of his work was not to be appreciated for many years. Einstein's theory of relativity had won him the Nobel Prize for Physics in 1921. Although few could understand its importance outside the scientific community, both the man and his work did catch the public imagination.

△ The introduction of dial telephones, pioneered in Chicago, reduced the average time for connecting calls from 62 seconds to 27.

▷ In 1923, archaeologist Howard Carter uncovered the tomb of 18th dynasty Egyptian pharaoh Tutankhamen. Public interest in archaeology was stimulated both by the scale and splendour of the finds and the sensational news coverage of the sudden death of Carter's patron, the Earl of Carnarvon. "Curse of the Pharaohs" screamed the headlines.

△ (Sir) Alexander Fleming, discoverer of penicillin, seen here at his work-bench in St. Mary's Hospital, Paddington.

(Inset) A massively enlarged image of *Penicillium notatum*. It was Fleming's second major discovery.

▷ John Logie Baird gave the world's first public demonstration of television in Soho, London on 26 January, 1926, transmitting the image of a ventriloquist's dummy. Baird was one of the last of the great inventors, working alone with primitive materials and home-made equipment, trying to turn a brilliant hunch into practical technology. Although hailed as "the father of television", Baird was to be bitterly disappointed by the ultimate decision of the BBC to drop his system when it began its public broadcasting services, a decade later.

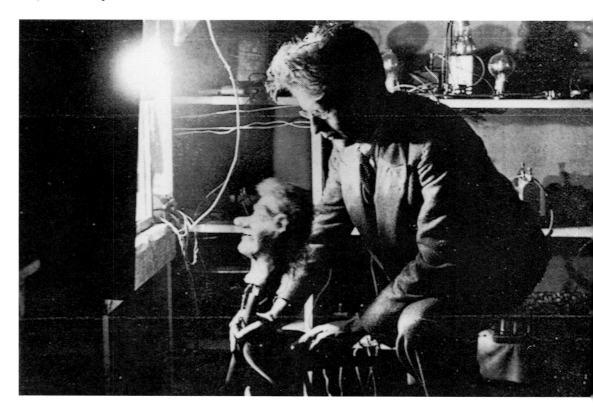

Art and Design

Design increasingly distinguished itself from art in the course of the decade. In 1919, the celebrated "Bauhaus" design school opened in Germany with architect Walter Gropius as its first director.

1920 saw the first publication of the avant-garde magazine *L'Esprit Nouveau (The New Spirit)* founded by the Swiss architect Le Corbusier. In 1928 came *Domus*, an Italian journal devoted to design. In the same year, France set up the Ecole de la Chambre Syndicale de la Couture to teach the skills of the high fashion industry.

Advances in new technology and research methods also opened up new possibilities. In 1926, the American chemicals giant Du Pont launched a wide range of synthetic paint colours. In the same year, the Berlei company produced a range of underwear based on a scientific analysis of body types.

▽ **Folding draught screens – a blend of modern and traditional design.**

▷ **A poster for the influential Bauhaus design school by Paul Klee.**

▽ **Refrigerators were still a luxury for the rich. Note the servant's uniform and the bottle of champagne on the bottom shelf.**

Four-fold Draught Screens—covered in Canvas of various shade

Browns, Blues, Black, Grey, Wine colour, Red, etc.   Height 5 ft. 8 in.

These delightful Screens are decorated in various ways.

No. 281/29.
Tops mounted with the charming "Old London Cries" prints.
Price .. **£4 14 6**

No. 282/29.
Mounted with copies of "Morland" pictures.
Price .. **£4 14 6**

Decorated wit

Pr

11335

Mahogany Colour and Carved Gilt Table Standard, wired 3 yds. flexible wire and key switch holder complete.

Price - £3 15 0

Cretonne and Silk Shade 12 in. dia.

Price - £1 10 0

WARING & GILLOW
OXFORD STREET. W.I. LTD

◁ As more homes acquired electricity, demand for new appliances rose. This lamp would cost a worker's weekly wage.

△ The Paris Exhibition of 1925 proved to be the major artistic event of the decade popularising "art decoratif" – the style now known as "art deco".

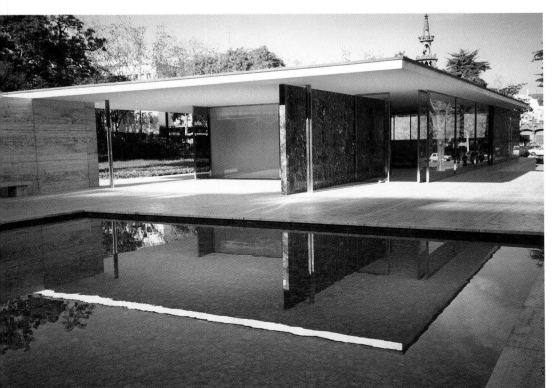

◁ The German Pavilion for the 1929 International Exhibition at Barcelona was a triumphant example of the style of the German-American architect Mies van der Rohe. A small one-storey building, it nevertheless demonstrated the basic elements he was to employ repeatedly – the use of richly coloured or textured materials, bold vertical and horizontal surfaces at right angles, transparent external walls and the use of load-bearing columns, freeing partitions to be disposed of at will. To furnish the Pavilion, Mies designed an equally distinctive chair, stool and glass-topped table.

Personalities of the 1920s

Baldwin, Stanley (1867–1947), three times Conservative Prime Minister of the United Kingdom.

Bondfield, Margaret (1873–1953), a teacher at the age of 13, she rose through the trade union movement to become the first woman chairman of the Trades Union Congress (TUC) in 1923 and, as Minister of Labour, Britain's first woman Cabinet Minister in 1929.

Bow, Clara (1905–65), American star of the silent screen whose appearance in *It* (1927) advertised a sex appeal which made her known as the "It Girl".

Bukharin, Nikolai (1888–1938), Russian co-author of the *ABC of Communism* and a member of the Politburo (1924–29) who fell from power after opposing the collectivization of agriculture and was executed in 1938.

Byrd, Richard (1888–1957), American naval aviator and explorer who flew over the North Pole in 1926. He also flew the Atlantic from west to east in 1927 and in 1929 flew over the South Pole.

Carter, Howard (1873–1939), English archaeologist in Egypt who uncovered the tomb of the Pharaoh Tutankhamen in 1922 and spent the next 10 years removing and recording its treasures.

Chaplin, Charlie (1889–1977), the world's first superstar as a result of such films as *The Kid* (1921).

Cobham, (Sir) Alan (1894–1973), British aviator knighted for his pioneering flights to establish safe air routes. In 1926 he flew around the world in 58 days.

Collins, Michael (1890–1922), tragic hero and first Prime Minister of the "Irish Free State". An ardent leader of the abortive 1916 "Easter Rising", he became a member of the first independent Irish parliament (Dail Eireann) and helped to negotiate the self-governing status of the 26 southern counties. He was assassinated by nationalists opposed to his acceptance of partition.

Dempsey, Jack (1895–1983), American world heavyweight boxing champion known as the "Manassa Mauler".

Eisenstein, Sergei Mikhailovich (1898–1948), Russian film director who chronicled the achievements of the Russian revolution while pioneering new cinematic techniques such as montage (editing and assembling pieces of film) and the "super close-up" in *The Battleship Potemkin* (1925) and *October* (1927).

Eliot, Thomas Stearns (1888–1965), American-born Oxford philosophy student who turned to poetry and supported himself by working in a bank. His unhappy marriage drove him to the edge of a breakdown but did not prevent him from completing *The Waste Land* which brought him fame in 1922. In 1927 he became a British subject.

Fairbanks, Douglas (1883–1939), American film star (born Julius Ullman) who starred in *The Mark of Zorro* (1920), *The Thief of Baghdad* (1924) and *The Black Pirate* (1926).

Gershwin, George (1898–1937), American songwriter and composer who combined traditional and jazz styles in his longer works *Rhapsody in Blue* (1924) and *An American in Paris* (1928).

Hemingway, Ernest (1899–1961), emerged as representative of the "lost generation" of Paris-based American expatriates with the publication of his novels *The Sun Also Rises* (1926) and *A Farewell to Arms* (1929). In 1954 he was awarded the Nobel Prize for Literature.

Hindenburg, Paul von (1847–1934), despite his advanced age, won spectacular victories during World War I to become a Field Marshal and national hero. Despite monarchist leanings, he supported the Weimar republic and was elected president (1925) and served as a much-needed symbol of stability and continuity.

Louis Armstrong

Margaret Bondfield

T. S. Eliot

Hitler, Adolf (1889–1945), as a disillusioned ex-soldier, Hitler was drawn into fringe politics, joining the German Workers Party which he transformed into the National Socialist (Nazi) party. An abortive coup attempt cost him a prison sentence but made him a national figure and helped place his party at the forefront of challenge to the shaky Weimar regime.

Houdini, Harry (1874–1926), Hungarian-born Ehrich Weiss renamed himself after a French magician, became an American citizen and won fame as a spectacular escapologist and exposer of fake mediums.

Lang, Fritz (1890–1976), Austrian-born film director whose *Metropolis* (1926) presented a frightening vision of the future and became an influential classic of cinematic technique.

Law, Andrew Bonar (1858–1923), Canadian-born Scottish businessman who became leader of the Conservative Party in 1911 and Prime Minister in 1922–3. Cancer forced the early resignation of "England's unknown Prime Minister" after a brief and ineffectual term of office.

Lenin, Vladimir Ilyich (1870–1924), creator of the Soviet Union and also of the Bolshevik party, which served many other revolutionary movements as a model of disciplined action.

Lewis, (Harry) Sinclair (1885–1951), American novelist who achieved fame with satires on the small town life of the American mid-west (*Main Street* (1920), *Babbitt* (1922)) and became the first American to win the Nobel Prize for Literature in 1930.

MacDonald, James Ramsay (1886–1937), twice Labour Prime Minister of the United Kingdom, he split his party by agreeing to head a "National Government" in 1931.

Mallory, George Leigh (1866–1924), led the first attempt on Mount Everest in 1921 and reached a record height the following year before being forced back by bad weather. He died on his third attempt, having been last seen alive a mere 800 feet below the summit.

Mussolini, Benito (1883–1945), creator of Fascist Italy whose regime served as a model for would-be right-wing revolutionaries throughout Europe.

Pickford, Mary (1893–1979), Canadian-born Gladys Smith became "America's Sweetheart" in films like *Tess of the Storm Country* (1922).

Shaw, George Bernard (1856–1950), Irish dramatist and social critic whose stature was confirmed by *Saint Joan* (1923) and the award of the Nobel Prize for Literature in 1925. He gave away the prize money. In 1928 he published *The Intelligent Woman's Guide to Socialism and Capitalism.*

Stopes, Marie (1880–1958), trained as a scientist and became a fervent promoter of birth control, opening Britain's first family-planning clinic in 1921 and gaining notoriety through such works as *Radiant Motherhood* (1920) and *Enduring Passion* (1928).

Stresemann, Gustav (1878–1929), German statesman who, as Chancellor (1923) and foreign minister (1923–9), struggled to establish his defeated country as a respected but co-operative European power. In 1926 he shared the Nobel Peace Prize with French statesman Aristide Briand (1862–1932).

Trotsky, Leon (1879–1940), Russian revolutionary, born Lev Davidovich Bronstein, who took the name of one of his jailers after escaping from Siberian exile. An advocate of world revolution, he was expelled from the party in 1927 and was murdered in his Mexican exile on Stalin's orders.

Paul von Hindenburg

Andrew Bonar Law

Gustav Stresemann

1920s Year by Year

1920

- Establishment of the League of Nations.
- Prohibition introduced in the United States.
- "Black and tans" active in Ireland.
- Nazi party established.
- French occupy the Ruhr.
- Treaty of Trianon dismembers the former Austro-Hungarian empire.
- League of Nations grants Britain a mandate over Palestine.
- Seventh Olympic games held in Antwerp.
- Russo-Polish war.
- Joan of Arc canonised as a saint.
- Communist Party of Great Britain established.
- 19th Amendment to the United States' Constitution gives women the right to vote in federal elections.
- Treaty of Sèvres dismembers the former Ottoman Empire.
- Bolsheviks defeat "Whites" and their Western supporters in Russia.
- Warren Harding elected President of the United States.
- Woodrow Wilson, outgoing American president, wins Nobel Peace Prize.
- First radio stations opened in America (KDKA, Pittsburgh) and Britain (Chelmsford).

1921

- Reza Khan seizes power in Persia.
- Unemployment exceeds 2 million in Britain.
- Sun Yat-sen elected President of China.
- Communist Party established in China.
- Mongolia declares itself independent as the world's second communist state.
- Kingdom of Iraq established.
- Famine in Russia's Volga region.

- Albert Einstein wins Nobel Prize for Physics.
- America, Britain, Japan and France sign Washington Treaty limiting naval armaments in the Pacific region.
- Insulin discovered as a treatment for diabetes.
- Johnson and Johnson introduce "Band-aid", the first stick-on bandage.
- Lie detector test invented.

1922

- Pius XI succeeds Benedict XV as Pope.
- Egypt proclaimed formally independent of Britain.
- First edition of *Reader's Digest* published.
- Assassination of Field Marshal Sir Henry Wilson; of German foreign minister Walther Rathenau and of Michael Collins, Commander in Chief of the Irish Free State Army.
- Fascist "March on Rome" puts Mussolini into power.
- Excavation of tomb of Egyptian Pharaoh Tutankhamen.
- Regular radio news broadcasts begin in Britain.

1923

- Hitler arrested after failure of a putsch in Munich.
- Mussolini dissolves all opposition parties in Italy.
- Earthquake destroys much of Tokyo and Yokohama.
- Civil disobedience campaign against British rule in India.
- Miguel Primo de Rivera leads army coup in Spain.
- Mustafa Kemal proclaims Turkey a republic with himself as President and moves the capital from Istanbul to Ankara.
- Collapse of German currency.
- First transatlantic radio broadcast and telephone call.

- British general election leads to minority Labour government.
- Wembley Stadium used for FA Cup Final for the first time.
- First successful in-flight re-fuelling.
- HMS *Hermes*, the world's first purpose-designed aircraft carrier, goes into service.
- Bulldozer is invented.

1924

- Death of Lenin – Petrograd renamed Leningrad in his honour.
- First Winter Olympics held at Chamonix, France.
- Death of Woodrow Wilson.
- First execution by gas chamber in the United States.
- Mustafa Kemal abolishes office of Caliph.
- Imperial Airways established as Britain's national airline.
- Greece votes to end its monarchy in favour of a republic.
- Metro-Goldwyn Mayer film corporation established.
- Assassination of Italian socialist leader Giacomo Matteotti.
- Dawes Plan agreed for German war reparations.
- Kimberley Clark introduce first disposable handkerchiefs – Celluwipes, later known as Kleenex.
- United States grants full citizenship to native American Indians.
- Calvin Coolidge elected president of the United States.

1925

- Mussolini assumes full dictatorial powers.
- Overthrow of governments in Chile, Portugal and Greece.
- Scope trial attracts national attention testing a Tennessee law banning the teaching of evolution in schools.

- Kurdish uprising suppressed in Turkey.
- Field Marshal von Hindenburg elected President of Germany.
- Exposition des Arts Décoratifs in Paris.
- Chiang Kai-shek succeeds Sun Yat-sen as leader of the Chinese Nationalist Party (Kuomintang).
- Chrysler Motor Company founded.
- Hitler's *Mein Kampf (My Struggle)* published.
- Locarno Treaty reaffirms the post-war European settlement.
- G. B. Shaw wins Nobel Prize for Literature and gives away the prize money.
- "Dipped" headlights introduced for cars.
- Battery cages for laying hens introduced in America.
- Crossword puzzles become popular.

1926

- Lufthansa airline founded in Germany.
- J. L. Baird demonstrates television.
- Safeways chain of general stores established in Maryland.
- Hindu-Muslim riots in India.
- Soviet-German friendship treaty.
- Reza Khan crowned as Shah of Persia.
- Nine day General Strike in Britain.
- Abd-al-Krim revolt in Morocco crushed.
- ICI formed as Britain's major chemicals manufacturer.
- Empire Prime Ministers meet in conference in London.
- Mussolini bans women from public offices and taxes bachelors.
- Hirohito becomes Emperor of Japan in his own right.
- Anti-freeze for car radiators allows all-year motoring.
- Zips replace buttons on jeans.
- First artificial ski-slope installed in London.
- Floyd Bennett and Richard Byrd fly over the North Pole.

- First pop-up toaster invented in the United States.
- American Gertrude Ederle becomes the first woman to swim the English channel.

1927

- British Broadcasting Corporation replaces British Broadcasting Company.
- London-Delhi air service begins.
- Major Segrave sets new world land-speed record.
- Chiang Kai-shek captures Shanghai.
- Lindbergh flies the Atlantic solo.
- Ahmed Sukarno founds the Indonesian Nationalist Party.
- Communist riots in Vienna leave 89 dead.
- First "talking picture", *The Jazz Singer*, exhibited.
- Stalin expels Trotsky and Zinoviev from the Soviet Communist Party.
- Babe Ruth hits 60 home runs for the New York Yankees.
- Wall-mounted can-opener introduced.
- First Volvo car manufactured.
- Prototype iron-lung incorporates parts from two old vacuum cleaners.
- Jerome Kern and Oscar Hammerstein II's *Showboat* opens in New York.

1928

- Britain gives women over 21 the vote.
- Turkey adopts the roman alphabet.
- Kellogg Pact outlaws war.
- Amelia Earhart becomes the first woman to fly the Atlantic.
- Geiger Counter invented.
- Fleming discovers penicillin.
- Chiang Kai-shek proclaimed President of China.
- Stalin issues Five Year Plan for economic development in the

Soviet Union.
- Eruption of Mount Etna.
- Herbert Hoover elected as President of the United States.
- "Flying Doctor" service introduced in Australia.
- "Rice Krispies" introduced.
- John Logie Baird demonstrates prototype video-disc.
- Quartz crystal clock invented – accurate to 1000th of a second per day.
- "Scotch tape" goes on sale in America.

1929

- Turkey adopts the metric system.
- U.S. Army plane flies 150 hours non-stop.
- St. Valentine's Day massacre of six Chicago gangsters.
- Mussolini signs Lateran Treaty establishing the Vatican state.
- "Oscar" awards established.
- Second Labour government comes to power in Britain.
- British declare martial law in Palestine.
- German airship *Graf Zeppelin* flies round the world in 21 days.
- Soviet-Chinese border clashes.
- French Premier Briand proposes a federal Europe.
- Wall Street crashes as New York Stock Exchange prices plunge.
- Britain's R101 launched as the world's biggest airship.
- American pilot Richard Byrd flies over the South Pole.
- Clarence Birdseye markets frozen foods.
- Kodak introduces 16mm colour movie film.
- Kitchen waste disposer introduced.
- Foam rubber produced.

Index